MW01227992

what is ANXIETY?

WRITTEN BY
RENETTA DANIELS

ILLUSTRATED BY
AMELIA SMITH

What is Anxiety
Copyright © 2023 by Renetta Daniels and Amelia Smith

Printed in United States of America
ISBN: 9798379365714
Imprint: Independently Published
Publication Date: 03/01/2023

Anxiety can cause you to worry.

Tony is starting a new school soon. He was worried about meeting new kids, new teachers, and being in a new class surrounded by strangers.

He thinks to himself, what if I get lost? Will I make new friends? What if no one likes me? What if the teacher isn't nice to me? What if everyone laughs at me? What if I take the wrong bus?

Tony feels his heart beating really fast and his legs trembling. His hands were really warm and shaking. He can't stop thinking about what could go wrong. He begins to panic.

Anxiety can make you feel very nervous.

Raven's parents are taking
her to her first dentist
appointment.

Raven is very nervous! She thinks, will it hurt? Will the dentist take all my teeth out ? How long will it take for me to grow new teeth? How will I eat my favorite foods?

Raven begins to sweat. She feels pains in her tummy. She begins to panic! She refuses to get out the car. She is too nervous to see the dentist. Raven closes her mouth tightly .

Anxiety can cause fear.

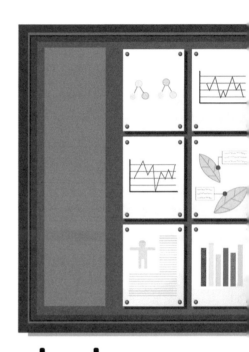

It is Mia's first day of preschool. She is excited to see all the fun new toys. She wears her favorite yellow dress with pink flowers.

Her parents walk Mia to her class and sign her in. Her teacher helps Mia wash her hands and shows her around the classroom.

Mia sees a beautiful doll and knows it will be her favorite.

Mia's parents give her a hug and kiss goodbye and walk to the door. She begs her parents not to leave her. Mia is afraid to be at preschool without her parents.

What if they are late coming back? What if they don't come back at all, she thought ? What if everyone goes home and leave her here all alone!

Mia tries standing in front of the door so her parents can't leave. When that doesn't work, she begins to cry uncontrollably begging them not to leave her. The tears soak the front of her beautiful yellow dress.

She falls to the floor grabbing her parents legs so they can't move.

Mia's parents pick her up and hug her tightly. They whisper to her softly until she begins to calm down. They let her know that she is safe as they stand at the door holding her. Her parents tell her teacher they will try again tomorrow.

Anxiety can cause you and your body to feel many different feelings. You may feel really nervous, scared, anxious, tense, overwhelmed, and may have stomach pains or even trouble sleeping.

Your body may start to feel weak, and your heart beat faster. You may shake, tremble, sweat, or experience fast breathing. It can be very scary and confusing. You may even feel like you don't have any control.

If you ever begin to feel like this,
you should talk to your parents.
Let them know exactly how you feel
and what you're thinking about.
Your parents can help you feel safe
and calm.

You can also get your favorite toy, play your favorite game, or read a book to help you calm down. Taking deep breaths, counting to ten, and counting backwards from ten can help reduce anxiety as well.

Going for a short walk with a friend or siblings can be helpful. There are many ways to help with anxiety such as taking a nap, exercising, eating healthy foods, writing in a notebook, coloring, drawing, or doing arts and crafts.

Anyone can have anxiety, at any age, for many reasons.

More books by Renetta Daniels

www.readingwithnetta.com

Made in the USA
Columbia, SC
28 February 2025

54526642R00024